# Friends

by Meg Greve

**Content Consultants:**
Melissa Z. Pierce, L.C.S.W.
Sam Williams, M.Ed.

Rourke
Educational Media
rourkeeducationalmedia.com

*Teacher Notes available at*
**rem4teachers.com**

www.rourkeeducationalmedia.com

Melissa Z. Pierce is a licensed clinical social worker with a background in counseling in the home and school group settings. Melissa is currently a life coach. She brings her experience as a L.C.S.W. and parent to the *Little World Social Skills* collection and the *Social Skills and More* program.

Sam Williams has a master's degree in education. Sam Williams is a former teacher with over 10 years of classroom experience. He has been a literacy coach, professional development writer and trainer, and is a published author. He brings his experience in child development and classroom management to this series.

PHOTO CREDITS: Cover: © Rosemarie Gearhart; page 3: © kali9; page 5: © Agnieszka Kirinicjanow; page 7: © Chris Bernard; page 9: © kali9; page 11: © Chris Bernard; page 13: © Cliff Parnell; page 15: © Aldo Murillo; page 17: © Jennifer Conner; page 19: © digitalskillet; page 21: © Steve Debenport

Illustrations by: Anita DuFalla

Edited by: Precious McKenzie

Cover and Interior designed by: Tara Raymo

## Library of Congress EPCN Data

Friends / Meg Greve
(Little World Social Skills)
ISBN 978-1-61810-129-7 (hard cover)(alk. paper)
ISBN 978-1-61810-262-1 (soft cover)
Library of Congress Control Number: 2011945273

Rourke Educational Media
Printed in the United States of America,
North Mankato, Minnesota

rourkeeducationalmedia.com

customerservice@rourkeeducationalmedia.com • PO Box 643328 Vero Beach, Florida 32964

What is a friend?

A friend is someone you can **trust**. Friends help each other. Friends **share**.

Friends talk to each other and like being together. Friends treat each other **fairly**.

7

How do you make a friend?

Be friendly and helpful. Use nice words and listen to others.

Friends don't call each other names.

Treat others how you want to be treated.

Treat people with **respect**.
Give everyone a chance.

Sometimes friends **argue.**

Friends say they are **sorry**. Then they stay friends. A friend likes you for who you are, no matter what!

We all make mistakes. Say "sorry" and mean it when you do.

# Take the Friendship Test!

1. I always try to treat my friends fairly. ⭕ yes ⭕ no

2. I share with my friends. ⭕ yes ⭕ no

3. My friends can trust me. ⭕ yes ⭕ no

4. I am a friend to others. ⭕ yes ⭕ no

5. I respect the feelings of others. ⭕ yes ⭕ no

# Picture Glossary

**argue** (AHR-gyoo):
To fight with words.

**fairly** (FAIR-lee):
Acting trustworthy and reasonably.

**respect** (ri-SPEKT):
A feeling of thoughtfulness and recognition that something is important.

**share** (SHAIR):
To divide equally and take turns.

**sorry** (SAHR-ee):
Feeling sad or bad about doing something wrong.

**trust** (TRUHST):
Believing that someone is honest and will do what is promised.

## Index

## Websites

www.kidsgen.com/events/friendshipday/facts.htm

www.singdancelearn.com/character-education-songs
 friend-song/

www.scholastic.com/cliffordbebig/kids/
 kids-slide-09.htm

## About the Author

Meg Greve lives with her husband, daughter, and son. Her family has lots of friends and loves to be with them!

**Ask The Author!**
www.rem4students.com